The Lost Son

Pictures by Denis Alonso

A man had a big farm.

He had two sons.

One son was named Jack.

Jack told his father,

"I do not want to work."

“I want to travel.

I want to have fun,”

said Jack.

“I want my part of the
family’s money,” Jack said.

Dad gave Jack some money.

Jack packed his clothes.

He packed a blanket.

Jack left his home.

“Good-bye! We love you,”
Dad said.

Jack went to the big city.

Jack had fun.

He ate fancy food.

He got fancy clothes.

Soon Jack's money
was all gone.

Jack got a job at a pig farm.

The farm was stinky!

Jack was hungry.
He wished he could eat
the pig's food.

Jack told the pigs,
"I want to go home."

Jack was never hungry before he left home.

“Maybe I can work for Dad.”

“Will Dad still love me?”

Jack asked.

Jack went all the way home.

Dad saw Jack.

Jack saw Dad.

Dad was happy to see Jack.

"I'm sorry, Dad," Jack said.

"I made a mistake.

I never should have left you."

“I forgive you, Jack,”
Dad said.

That night they had a party.

"I'm so happy you are home,"
said Dad.

“My son was lost.
Now he is found,” Dad said.